WELCOME TO THE WORLD

How Mary Has Kittens.

WELCOME TO

Written & illustrated by

Ann Sayre Wiseman

With sketches
and comments
by Amy 10
   Sylvia 8
   Octavia 7
   Alex 6

Text and illustrations Copyright © 1980
by Ann Sayre Wiseman
All Rights Reserved
Addison-Wesley Publishing Company, Inc.
Reading, Massachusetts 01867
Printed in the United States of America
ABCDEFGHIJK-WZ-89876543210

**Library of Congress Cataloging in
Publication Data**

Wiseman, Ann Sayre, 1926-

   Welcome to the world.

SUMMARY: Text and drawings record the con-
ception and birth of eight kittens.

   1. Cats--Reproduction--Juvenile litera-
ture. [1. Cats--Reproduction. 2. Birth]
I. Title.
SF445.7.W57   599'.74428   79-24819
ISBN 0-201-08575-5

 # ADDISON WESLEY

THE WORLD

How Mary Has Kittens

PETE'S CAT MARY IS A BEAUTIFUL TIGER

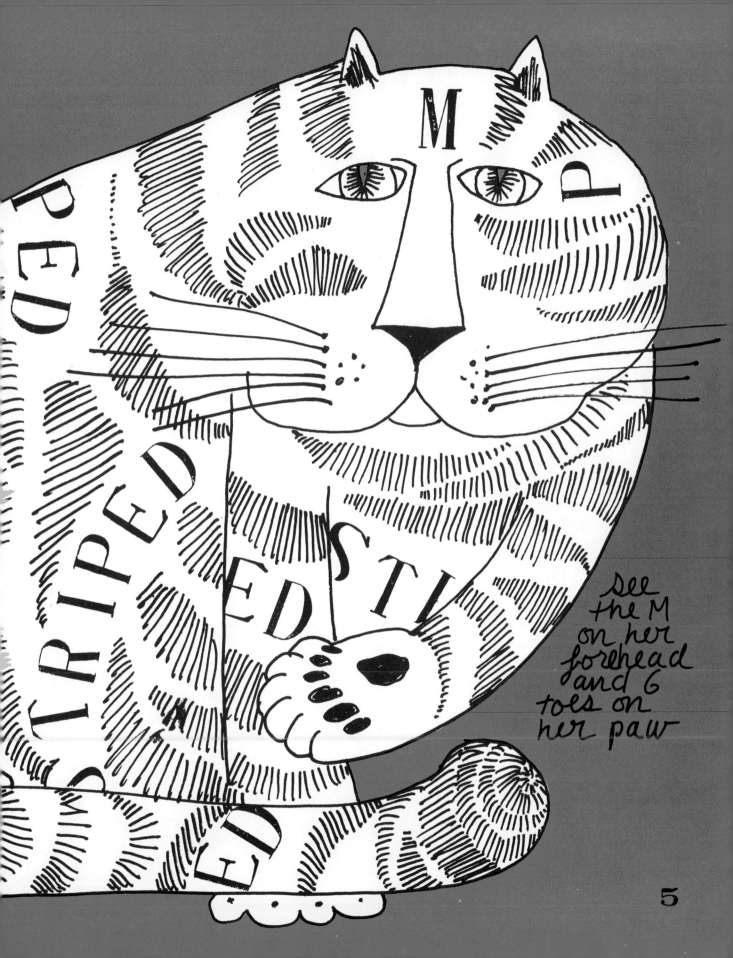

see the M on her forehead and 6 toes on her paw

5

MARY LOVES TO SLEEP ON PETE'S BED

7

WHEN MARY WAS OLD ENOUGH TO HAVE KITTENS SHE WENT OUT HUNTING FOR A MATE

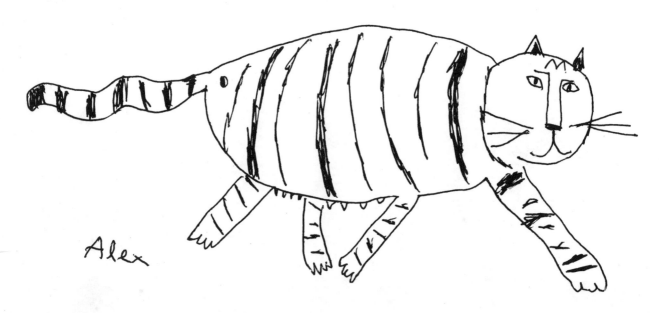

Alex

all the Tom cats were interested because Mary was <u>in heat</u>

That means she is ready to mate and become a mother

MARY
LIKES
SPOT

Spot thinks Mary has a good smell
that tells him she is ready
to mate and have babies

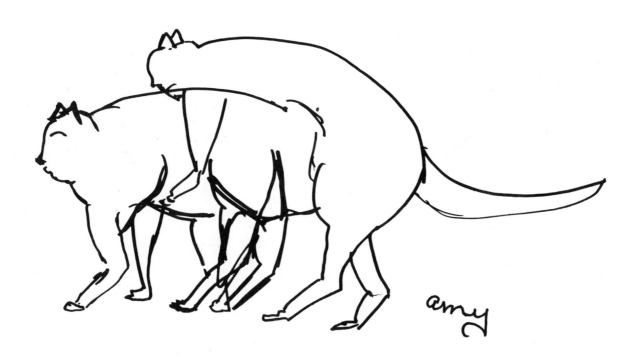

amy

Mary and Spot are mating

Sylvia

Spot puts sperm inside Mary

Alex

Mary is waiting for the babies to grow inside her belly

IT TAKES 9 WEEKS FOR KITTENS TO GROW BIG ENOUGH TO BE BORN

MARY
TAKES
GOOD
CARE OF
HER BODY

13

CAN YOU
GUESS
HOW MANY
KITTENS
MARY HAS
INSIDE

4

8

2

1

3

IF YOU PUT A GENTLE HAND ON HER TUMMY YOU CAN FEEL THE KITTENS

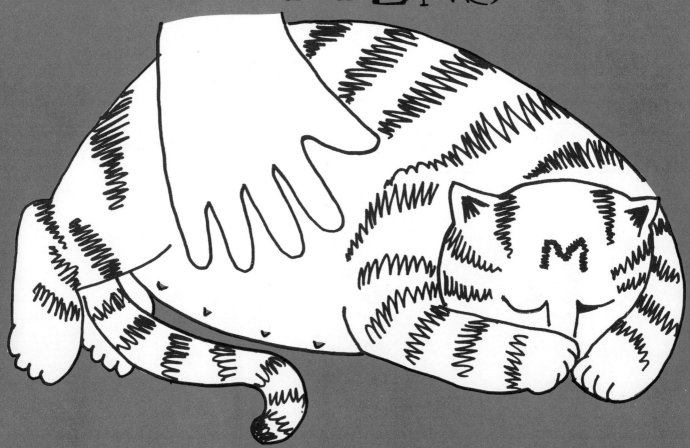

THIS IS NOT THE BEST WAY TO HOLD A PREGNANT CAT

ON THE 63rd DAY PETE & FRIENDS MADE READY A BOX FOR MARY'S BABIES

We waited all night to see how Mary had her babies so we could make pictures for this story.

NOTHING HAPPENED

LATE THAT NIGHT MARY DISAPPEARED PETE LOOKED EVERYWHERE

CLOSET

CELLAR

ATTIC

COUCH

TUB

MAYBE SHE WANTS
TO BE PRIVATE

21

BEFORE DAWN PETE HEARD A NOISE UNDER HIS BED

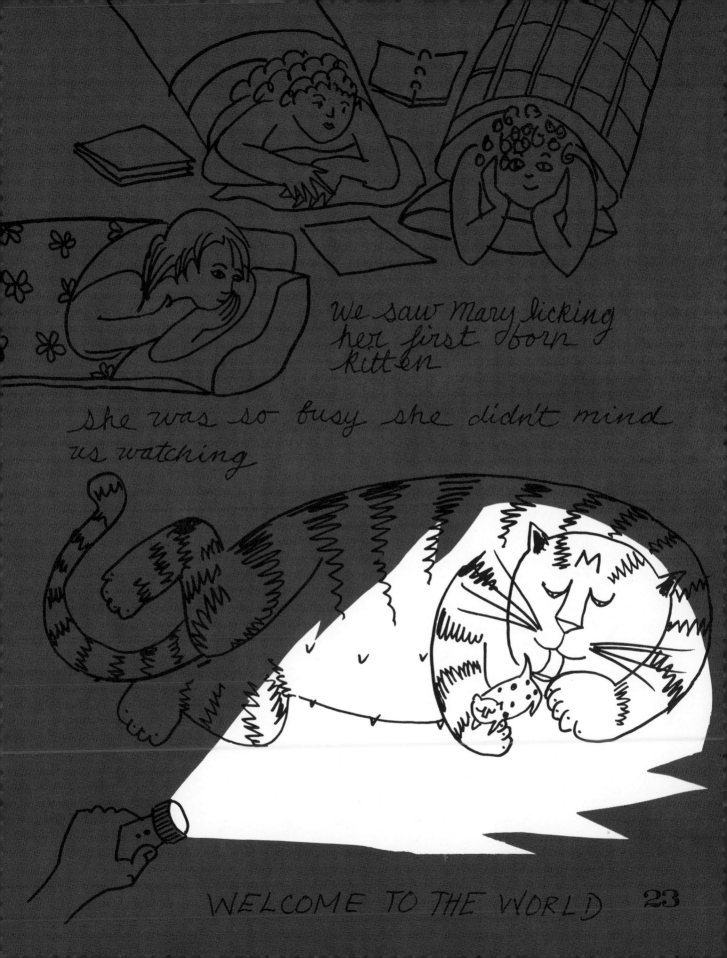

We saw Mary licking her first born kitten

she was so busy she didn't mind us watching

WELCOME TO THE WORLD   23

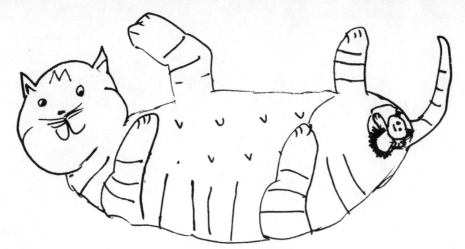

This is how a kitten is born

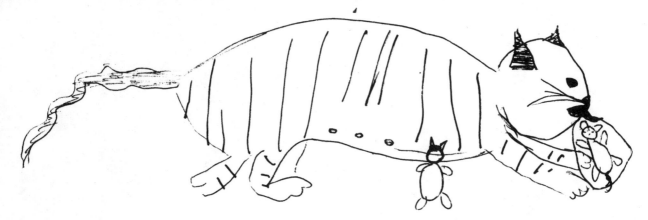

gets licked and fluffed up

Syloia

sometimes babies are born feet first

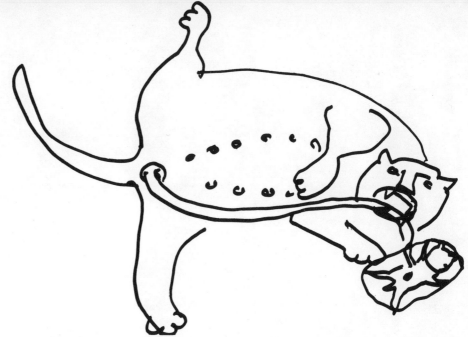

mary is biting off the umbilical cord
because the baby doesn't need it
after it is born

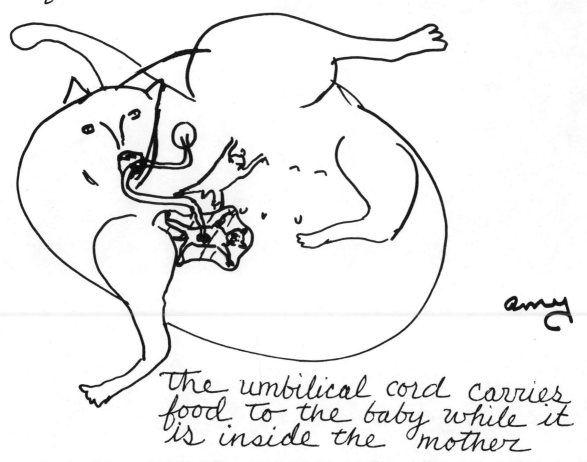

the umbilical cord carries
food to the baby while it
is inside the mother

FINALLY THE LAST KITTEN IS BORN

every one is different

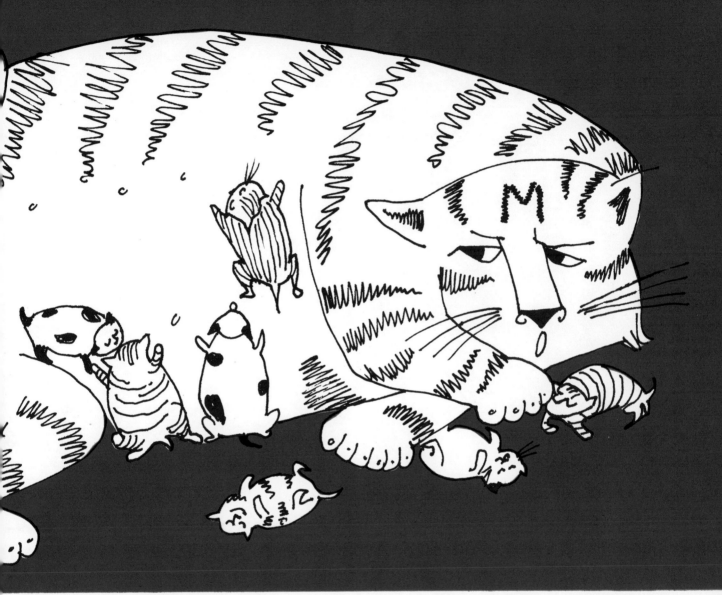

would you like to give them names

8 kittens are sucking milk from 8 ripples

everybody is happy

29

Mary carries her kittens in her mouth
to the box to keep them safe
until they are old enough to take
care of themselves

Alex

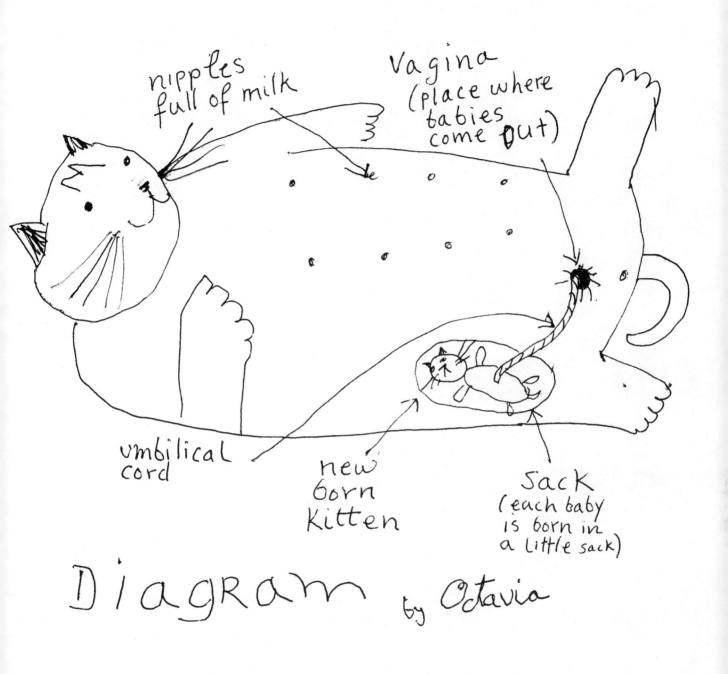

nipples
full of milk

Vagina
(place where
babies
come out)

umbilical
cord

new
born
Kitten

Sack
(each baby
is born in
a little sack)

Diagram by Octavia

All babies are born this way
including you and me

THE END

THE BEGINNING

for Piet * *